AND
CHILTERNS
RECIPES

Compiled by Dorothy Baldock

*with illustrations by
Sutton Palmer RA*

SALMON

Index

Aylesbury Game Pie 27
Aylesbury Roast Duck 19
Beef Stew with Walnuts 32
Berkshire Hog 8
Berkshire Jugged Steak 24
Braised Liver with Raisins etc. 29
Buckingham Bacon Badger 5
Buckingham Cakes 34
Buckinghamshire Cherry Dumpers 37
Buckinghamshire Dumpling 16
Buckinghamshire Rabbit Pie 45
Chiltern Hills Pudding 21
Devilled Mutton 35
Duke of Windsor's Gingerbread 46
Eton Mess 42
Gammon and Apricot Pie 39
Her Majesty's Pudding 15

Hollygog Pudding 3
Lamb in Devil Sauce 14
Little Mutton Pies 31
Orange Tart 43
Oxford John 26
Oxford Marmalade 7
Oxford Sausages 38
Pancakes 47
Poor Knights of Windsor 23
Ragout of Lamb 22
Rout Biscuits 11
Rout Cakes 30
Spiced Oxford Cake 13
Sweet Cake 18
White Windsor Soup 10
Windsor Castle Cake 6
Windsor Tartlets 40

Cover pictures: *front:* Harvest at Pitstone *by Stephen Cubitt*
Back: Watermeadows by the Thames *by H. Taplin*
Title page: The Cross, East Hagbourne

Hollygog Pudding

A farmhouse roly-poly pudding, said to have been first made in the Oxfordshire village of Kiddington near Woodstock.

8 oz flour	4 tablespoons golden syrup, warmed
Pinch of salt	
4 oz butter	1 teaspoon lemon juice, optional
3 to 4 tablespoons water	½ pint milk
A little extra butter	

Set oven to 400°F or Mark 6. Sift the flour and salt into a bowl, then rub in the butter until the mixture resembles fine breadcrumbs. Add sufficient water to form a stiff dough, then turn out on to a lightly floured surface and roll out into a rectangle between ⅛ to ¼ inch in thickness. Spread the syrup over the pastry, then sprinkle over the lemon juice, if desired. Roll up like a Swiss Roll and place in a well buttered ovenproof dish. Pour over sufficient milk to come halfway up the side of the pudding and dot the top with a little extra butter. Bake for 30 to 40 minutes and serve, cut into slices, with custard or cream. Serves 4 to 6.

Brill Windmill

Buckingham Bacon Badger

This boiled pudding is a traditional country way of extending a relatively small amount of meat and the Buckinghamshire version is always known as a 'badger' because of its well rounded badger-like shape.

1 lb bacon, derinded and chopped	2 teaspoons chopped fresh sage
1 onion, peeled and finely chopped	Black pepper
1 potato, peeled and finely diced	8 oz prepared suet crust pastry

Mix together the bacon, onion, potato and sage and season well with pepper. Roll out the pastry on a lightly floured surface to form a rectangle about 12 inches by 9 inches. Spread the bacon mixture over the pastry, leaving about ½ inch around the edges. Dampen the edges, then roll up like a Swiss roll and press the ends together firmly. Wrap up in a clean, well floured pudding cloth and then wrap again in kitchen foil. Tie the ends tightly, but allow the pudding room to expand. Place in a saucepan of boiling water and boil for 2½ to 3 hours, topping up the water if necessary. Serve cut into thick slices, accompanied by thick, brown gravy, boiled potatoes and a green vegetable. Serves 4 to 6.

If preferred, though it is not traditional, the Badger can be made by lining a greased pudding basin with the pastry, then adding the filling and a pastry lid and steaming for the same length of time.

Windsor Castle Cake

A cake containing ground rice and lemon rind, somewhat on the lines of a Madeira.

4 oz flour	8 oz caster sugar
$\frac{1}{2}$ teaspoon baking powder	Grated rind of a lemon
6 oz ground rice	2 eggs, beaten
8 oz butter	$\frac{1}{2}$ pint milk

A little sifted icing sugar

Set oven to 350°F or Mark 4. Sift the flour and baking powder together into a bowl, then add the ground rice. Rub in the butter until the mixture resembles fine breadcrumbs, then stir in the sugar and lemon rind. Add the eggs, combining well, then stir in sufficient milk to produce a soft, dropping consistency. Turn into a well greased and base lined 7 inch round cake tin and bake for 2 hours, until well risen and golden, covering the top with a piece of kitchen foil if it appears to be browning too quickly. Cool in the tin for 5 minutes, then turn out and place on a wire rack. Before serving, dust the top with a little sifted icing sugar.

Oxford Marmalade

A dark chunky preserve which at one time included ginger and black treacle.

3 lb Seville oranges   1 small lemon   6 pints water   6 lb preserving sugar

Wipe and peel the oranges and lemon and cut the peel into strips about 1 to 1½ inches long and ⅛ inch wide; adjusted to suit individual taste. Cut the flesh into small pieces and reserve the pips. Put the peel and fruit into a large bowl and pips into a small one. Bring 6 pints of water to the boil. Pour 5 pints over the peel and fruit and the remaining pint over the pips. Cover both bowls and leave to stand overnight. Next day the pips will be covered in a soft jelly. Lift the pips out of the water and place in a sieve set over a bowl. Pour the pip water over the pips to wash off the jelly; repeat until pips are clean. Discard pips and pour the jelly water into the fruit water. Pour peel, fruit and water into a preserving pan, bring to the boil and continue boiling until the peel is very soft - about 45 to 60 minutes. The longer the mixture boils the darker the finished marmalade. When the peel is soft, remove from heat and add the sugar, stirring until dissolved. Bring slowly back to boil and boil gently until marmalade has become as dark as required. Then boil rapidly for 15 minutes. Test for 'set' and when setting point is reached, remove from the heat and skim surface with a slotted spoon. Stand for 15 minutes, then stir to distribute peel evenly. Pour into clean, dry, warm jars, cover and label. Makes about 9 lb.

Berkshire Hog

The county of Berkshire is the home of the Black Berkshire breed of pig.

4 pork chops, wiped and trimmed
1 oz butter
1 tablespoon oil
2 sprigs parsley, 1 sprig thyme,
   1 sage leaf and a bayleaf,
   tied together with string

$^1/_2$ pint white wine or pork stock
8 button onions, peeled
4 oz mushrooms, wiped and sliced
1 tablespoon flour
$^1/_4$ pint single cream
Salt and black pepper

Parsley sprigs for garnish

Heat the butter and oil together in a pan, then add the pork chops and brown lightly on both sides. Remove the chops, add the onions and cook gently until golden. Add the wine or stock and *bouquet garni* and return the chops to the pan. Bring to the boil, then cover and simmer gently for 45 minutes to 1 hour. Add the mushrooms and cook for a further 10 minutes. Blend the flour with a little of the cream. Remove the pan from the heat and stir in the flour mixture. Bring back to the boil and boil for 1 minute. Stir in the remainder of the cream and the seasoning and heat through, but do not allow to boil. Remove and discard the *bouquet garni* and serve, garnished with parsley sprigs and accompanied by creamed potatoes, carrots and a green vegetable. Serves 4.

Sonning Bridge

White Windsor Soup

*Very different from the meat-based Brown Windsor Soup, White Windsor Soup
was a particular favourite of Queen Victoria.*

2 oz butter	2 pints chicken stock
1½ lb potatoes, peeled and chopped	4 sprigs parsley, 2 sprigs thyme and a bayleaf, tied with string
1 large onion, peeled and chopped	Salt and black pepper
2 sticks of celery, trimmed and chopped	½ pint milk
	1 oz cornflour
	A little milk

Fresh chopped parsley or watercress leaves for garnish

Melt the butter in a large saucepan. Add the potato, onion and celery, cover and cook for 5 to 10 minutes, without browning. Add the stock, *bouquet garni* and seasoning, bring to the boil and then simmer until the vegetables are tender. Allow to cool a little, remove the herbs then purée in a processor or liquidizer. Blend the cornflour to a smooth cream with a little milk. Pour the soup into a clean saucepan and add the milk. Stir well and bring to the boil, then add the cornflour mixture. Heat the soup through and adjust the seasoning if necessary. Serve garnished with parsley or watercress and accompanied by triangles of toast. Serves 4.

Rout Biscuits

These sweetmeats were popular accompaniments to a glass of wine or sherry at routs or fashionable gatherings in the 18th and 19th centuries. A Middlesex recipe.

6 oz caster sugar　　　**A few drops of almond or**
6 oz ground almonds　　**ratafia essence**
2 egg whites　　　　　**A little beaten egg yolk**
Small pieces of glacé cherry,angelica or flaked almonds for decoration

Set oven to 350ºF or Mark 4. In a bowl, combine the sugar and ground almonds together until evenly coloured. Gradually stir in the egg whites, stirring until the mixture is smooth and firm. Spoon into a piping bag fitted with a small rosette, star or scroll nozzle. Setting the biscuits well apart on a greased baking sheet, pipe each one according to inclination. Decorate with a piece of cherry, angelica or flaked almond, brush lightly with beaten egg yolk to give a golden glaze and bake for 6 to 7 minutes. Cool on a wire rack.

The Thames at Abingdon

Spiced Oxford Cake

A dark cake containing raisins, peel, spice and treacle.

10 oz flour	**8 oz raisins or sultanas**
$^1/_2$ teaspoon baking powder	**3 oz chopped mixed peel**
$^3/_4$ teaspoon mixed spice	**2 oz black treacle, warmed slightly**
6 oz butter	**Juice of half a lemon**
6 oz soft brown sugar	**5 fl. oz milk**

Set oven to 350°F or Mark 4. Sift the flour, baking powder and spice together into a bowl and then rub in the butter until the mixture resembles fine breadcrumbs. Stir in the sugar, fruit and peel. Mix the treacle and lemon juice together and stir into the mixture and then add sufficient milk to give a dropping consistency. Turn the mixture into a greased and base lined 8 inch round cake tin and bake for 1¾ to 2 hours, covering the top with a piece of kitchen foil if it appears to be browning too quickly. Allow to cool in the tin for 5 minutes, then turn out on to a wire rack.

Lamb in Devil Sauce

*Cold lamb simmered in a devil sauce. A light luncheon or
supper dish from Buckinghamshire.*

2 oz butter
1 small onion, peeled and
  very finely chopped
2 tablespoons white wine vinegar
3 tablespoons redcurrant jelly
1/2 teaspoon French mustard

Salt and black pepper
1/2 teaspoon cayenne pepper
1 dessertspoon finely chopped
  fresh parsley
8 slices cold roast lamb
1 tablespoon tomato purée

Parsley sprigs for garnish

Melt the butter in a frying pan and fry the onion until soft. Add the vinegar and
redcurrant jelly and simmer, stirring, until the jelly has melted. Stir in the
mustard, salt and pepper, cayenne pepper and parsley. Add the lamb slices and
simmer gently for 5 minutes, or until the meat is fully heated through. If the
sauce appears to be thickening too much, add 1 to 2 dessertspoons of stock.
Remove the lamb from the sauce and arrange on a heated dish. Stir the tomato
purée into the sauce and heat through thoroughly. Spoon over the lamb and
serve garnished with parsley sprigs and accompanied by boiled potatoes and
green peas. Serves 4.

Her Majesty's Pudding

A vanilla flavoured custard-cream pudding from Windsor.

1 oz butter	1 pint milk or single cream
5 eggs	A few drops of vanilla essence
2 oz caster sugar	A thin strip of lemon peel
	Grated nutmeg

Use ½ oz butter to grease a 1½ pint ovenproof dish. Beat the eggs and sugar together in a bowl until the sugar has dissolved. Heat the milk or cream in saucepan with the vanilla essence and lemon peel, until just boiling. Leave to infuse for 30 minutes, then bring back to the boil again. Allow to cool a little, then remove the lemon peel and pour on to the egg mixture, stirring continuously. Strain the mixture into the prepared dish, dot with the remaining butter and sprinkle with nutmeg. Set oven to 325°F or Mark 3. Place the dish in a roasting tin, pour in sufficient boiling water to come halfway up the side of the dish and bake for 35 to 40 minutes. In order to brown the top, place the pudding on the top shelf of the oven for 2 to 3 minutes. Serve hot or cold with fresh fruit accompanied by whipped cream. Serves 4 to 6.

Buckinghamshire Dumpling

A suet roly-poly containing bacon, liver and onions.

1 lb prepared suet pastry
8 oz streaky bacon rashers, derinded
8 oz pig's or lamb's liver, wiped and sliced

2 onions, peeled and finely chopped
2 teaspoons chopped fresh parsley
1 teaspoon chopped sage

Pepper

Roll out the pastry on a lightly floured surface to form a square about ¼ inch thick. Lay the bacon rashers on top, then cover with liver slices. Mix together the onion and herbs, season with pepper and sprinkle over the liver. Dampen the edges, then roll up like a Swiss roll and press the ends together. Wrap in a clean, well floured pudding cloth, then wrap again in kitchen foil. Tie the ends tightly, but allow the dumpling room to expand. Place in a saucepan of boiling water and boil for 2½ to 3 hours, topping up the water if necessary. Unwrap and serve cut into slices, accompanied by creamed potatoes and a rich brown gravy. Serves 4 to 6.

An Old Corner, Chenies

Sweet Cake

An 18th century recipe that comes from Reading in Berkshire.

6 oz butter, softened **8 oz flour**
4 oz caster sugar   **3 tablespoons brandy**
3 eggs and 2 egg yolks, **3 tablespoons sherry**
 beaten together   **A little sifted icing sugar**

Set oven to 350°F or Mark 4. Butter and line an 8 inch round cake tin. In a bowl, cream together the butter and sugar until light and fluffy, then beat in the beaten eggs. Add the flour a little at a time, beating well between each addition. Mix together the brandy and sherry and stir in, a little at a time, combining well. Turn the mixture into the prepared tin and bake for 1 hour, covering the top with a piece of kitchen foil if it appears to be browning too quickly. Cool in the tin for 5 minutes before turning out on to a wire rack. Finally, before serving, dust the top with a little sifted icing sugar.

Aylesbury Roast Duck

The handsome, true white Aylesbury duck is the best of British breeds.

1 oven-prepared duck, about 5 lb   A little butter   Salt - ideally sea salt

ORANGE SAUCE

Rind and juice of 2 oranges   2 tablespoons redcurrant jelly
½ pint duck giblet stock   2 tablespoons brandy
4 tablespoons duck juices   Salt and black pepper
**   from the roasting tin   1 orange, sliced and a few**
1 tablespoon brown sugar   watercress sprigs for garnish

Set oven to 375°F or Mark 5. Prick the duck all over with a fork, then rub with butter and sprinkle with salt. Place in a tin and roast, allowing about 20 minutes to the lb plus an extra 15 minutes and baste occasionally. Boil the duck neck and giblets with a small piece of celery, carrot and onion to make the stock. Remove the duck from the roasting tin, reserving the juices, place on a hot dish and keep warm. *Orange Sauce*; place the orange rind and juice in a saucepan and add ½ pint of strained stock. Strain the pan juices and add about 4 tablespoons, with the sugar, redcurrant jelly and brandy. Stir until all are fully dissolved, then season and heat through thoroughly. Pour a little over the duck, garnish with orange slices and watercress sprigs and serve with roast potatoes and green peas and the remainder of the sauce. Serves 4.

Nineteen

Cliveden Woods near Maidenhead

Chiltern Hills Pudding

A steamed pudding containing dried fruit, suet and tapioca.

2 oz tapioca	1 teaspoon bicarbonate of soda
¼ pint milk	dissolved in a little milk
1 tablespoon single cream	4 oz fresh white breadcrumbs
4 oz shredded suet	3 oz sugar
4 oz raisins or sultanas	A few drops of vanilla essence

In a bowl, soak the tapioca in the milk for 2 hours, then stir in the cream. Mix together the suet and the dried fruit. Add the bicarbonate of soda to the tapioca, then stir in the suet mixture, breadcrumbs, sugar and vanilla essence. Mix well together and turn into a well buttered 2 to 2½ pint putting basin. Cover with greaseproof paper and kitchen foil and seal. Place in a saucepan and add sufficient boiling water to come half way up the side of the basin, cover and steam for 2½ to 3 hours, topping up the water as necessary. Turn out on a warm serving dish and serve with cream, custard or vanilla sauce. Serves 4 to 6.

Ragout of Lamb

Ragouts, or rich stews, were popular from the 16th century - this is a Berkshire recipe.

1 breast of lamb
2 oz butter
1 to 1½ pints lamb stock
1 onion, peeled and left whole
15 cloves
3 carrots, peeled and finely sliced
4 oz mushrooms, sliced
A walnut of butter

2 teaspoons lemon juice
4 sprigs parsley, 1 sprig thyme,
  1 small sprig rosemary and
  a bayleaf tied together with string
Salt and black pepper
4 tablespoons cooked broad beans
  or peas or frozen peas
Fresh chopped parsley for garnish

Cut the lamb into cubes, removing as much fat as possible and dust with seasoned flour. Melt the butter and fry the lamb until golden. Heat the stock in a large saucepan. Stick the onion with the cloves, add to the stock and bring to the boil. Add the meat, cover and simmer for 30 minutes. Lightly brown the carrots in the residual butter and add to the meat, together with the *bouquet garni* and simmer for 1½ to 2 hours, stirring from time to time. Lightly fry the mushrooms in the walnut of butter and lemon juice. Season and add to the meat together with the broad beans or peas. Remove the herbs and the onion and cook for a further 10 to 15 minutes. Serve, garnished with chopped parsley and creamed potatoes. Serves 4 to 6.

Poor Knights of Windsor

A traditional Berkshire pudding based on the medieval French dish Pain Perdu or Lost Bread. The name is said to refer to the elderly pensioner-knights who lived in lodgings in Windsor in the Middle Ages.

6 thick slices white bread	**2 tablespoons sherry**
2 eggs	**Pinch of cinnamon**
2 teaspoons caster sugar	**Finely grated rind of half a lemon**
1/4 pint milk or single cream	**Butter and oil for frying**

Extra cinnamon and sugar for sprinkling

Remove the crusts from the bread and cut each slice into 3 fingers. In a bowl, beat the eggs and sugar together. Heat the milk or cream in a pan until it is almost boiling, then allow to cool a little. Pour into the egg mixture and beat well. Stir in the cinnamon, lemon rind and sherry. Melt the butter and oil together in a frying pan. Dip the fingers of bread into the egg mixture and fry until crisp and golden. Drain on kitchen paper and keep warm. Sprinkle with a mixture of cinnamon and sugar and serve at once, accompanied by warm apricot jam. Serves 4 to 6.

Berkshire Jugged Steak

A simple, but delicious recipe that has its origins in the cauldron cookery of the Middle Ages, when a number of different dishes were boiled together in one large pot.

1½ to 2 lb rump steak	**Salt and black pepper**
1 onion, peeled and left whole	**1 or 2 teaspoons mushroom ketchup**
10 cloves	**3 sprigs parsley and**
2 carrots, peeled and diced	**a small bayleaf,**
2 sticks celery, trimmed and diced	**tied together with string**

Cut the steak into small, neat cubes and place in a tall narrow casserole that has been rinsed out in cold water. Stick the onion with the cloves and add to the meat. Rinse the carrots and celery in cold water, drain well and add to the meat. Season, then add the mushroom ketchup and *bouquet garni*. Do *not* add any fat, stock or water. Cover the casserole with a piece of kitchen foil and place the lid firmly on top. Place in a saucepan of boiling water and stew for 2 hours, topping up the water as necessary. Before serving, discard the herbs and the cloves from the onion and then slice the onion and return it to the casserole. Serve with boiled potatoes and a green vegetable. Serves 4 to 6.

East Garston, Lambourn Valley

Oxford John

A quickly prepared dish of fresh lamb fried in herbs. Originally it was made with thick slices cut from a fresh leg of lamb or mutton.

4 lamb steaks approx. 6 oz each	2 shallots, peeled and finely chopped
1 teaspoon fresh chopped parsley	1 oz butter
1/2 teaspoon fresh chopped thyme	1/2 oz flour
1/2 teaspoon fresh chopped mint	1/2 pint lamb stock
Pinch of ground mace	Juice of half a lemon
Salt and black pepper	Croutons

Wipe the lamb steaks with a piece of kitchen paper. Mix together the herbs, spice, seasoning and shallots and coat the lamb steaks lightly with this mixture, pressing down well. Melt the butter in a frying pan and fry the steaks gently, turning occasionally until cooked through. Remove with a slotted spoon and place on a warm serving dish. Stir the flour into the remaining butter in the pan and cook, stirring, for 1 minute, then gradually add the stock and lemon juice. Bring to the boil, stirring, and simmer for 2 minutes. Return the steaks to the pan and simmer for a further 5 minutes. Serve garnished with croutons and accompanied by creamed potatoes and a green vegetable. Serves 4.

Aylesbury Game Pie

A rich pie, particularly popular in Victorian and Edwardian times.

**1 oz butter   4 prepared pigeons   1 onion, peeled and chopped
¹/₄ pint beef stock   4 tablespoons sherry   2 oz salt belly port
3 oz fresh white breadcrumbs   8 oz minced beef or veal
4 tablespoons chopped parsley   Black pepper   Grated rind of half a lemon
1 dessertspoon brandy   12 oz prepared shortcrust pastry   Beaten egg to glaze**

Melt butter in saucepan and brown pigeons all over. Add onion, cook for 1 minute then pour over stock and sherry. Bring to boil, cover and simmer for 50 minutes. Remove pigeons, reserving stock. Place pork in saucepan, cover with cold water, bring to boil and simmer until tender. Drain, cool, then mince coarsely. Mix with the breadcrumbs, the pork, beef or veal, parsley, pepper, lemon rind and brandy. Add stock to bind mixture. Remove pigeon meat from bones. Set oven to 400°F or Mark 6. Roll out pastry and use two thirds to line well greased raised pie mould. Place layer of pigeon meat on base, then layer breadcrumb mixture and pigeon meat alternately, finishing with layer of breadcrumbs. Cover with the remaining pastry, seal edges and make a steam hole. Decorate. Brush with beaten egg and bake for 1 hour, then lower oven to 350°F or Mark 4 and bake for further 30 minutes, covering with kitchen foil if browning too quickly. Carefully remove pie from mould, brush with the remaining beaten egg and return to oven for further 10 minutes. Serve hot or cold. Serves 4 to 6.   *Twenty-seven*

The Thames Valley at Bourne End

Braised Liver with Raisins and Almonds

A Buckinghamshire recipe.

2 oz butter
2 small onions, peeled and sliced
1½ lb lamb's liver, wiped and
    cut into ½ inch slices
1 oz flour

2 oz seedless raisins or sultanas
1 teaspoon fresh chopped thyme
¼ pint red wine
1 pint lamb stock
Salt and black pepper

3 oz blanched almonds, chopped

Melt 1 oz butter in a frying pan and fry the onions until soft. Butter a shallow, ovenproof casserole dish. Dust the liver slices with flour and lay half of them in the casserole. Place the onions on top and sprinkle over half the raisins and all the thyme, then top with the remaining liver and raisins. Mix together the wine and stock and season. Pour over the liver. Cover and allow to stand for 10 minutes. Set oven to 350°F or Mark 4 and cook for 1 to 1½ hours. Fry the almonds in the remaining 1 oz of butter until golden. Remove the casserole from the oven and sprinkle over the almonds. Return to the oven and cook, uncovered, for 5 minutes. Serve with creamed potatoes, carrots and a green vegetable. Serves 4 to 6.

Rout Cakes

Like Rout Biscuits and also from Middlesex, these cakes were eaten at fashionable gatherings or routs.

8 oz flour	**1 oz currants**
¹/₂ to ³/₄ oz butter	**2 fl. oz brandy**
2 oz caster sugar	**A few drops orange flower water**
2 oz candied orange and lemon peel, mixed	**2 small eggs, beaten**
	A little sifted icing sugar

Set oven to 425°F or Mark 7. Sift the flour into a bowl, then rub in the butter. Stir in the sugar, peel and currants and then add the brandy and orange flower water. Mix to a soft, dropping consistency with sufficient of the beaten egg (all of it may not be required) and place teaspoons of the mixture, set well apart, on a greased baking sheet. Bake for 10 minutes until golden. Cool on a wire rack and dust lightly with sifted icing sugar before serving.

Little Mutton Pies

A 19th century recipe, served at dinners given by the Duke of Buckingham.

¼ pint red wine	1 teaspoon chopped fresh thyme
½ pint lamb stock	1 teaspoon chopped fresh parsley
12 oz lean lamb, finely chopped	Salt and black pepper
1 onion, peeled and finely chopped	1 lb prepared puff pastry
8 oz mushrooms, finely chopped	1 beaten egg for glazing

Boil the wine in a large saucepan until it is reduced by one third, then stir in the stock. Add the lamb, onion, mushrooms, herbs and seasoning, bring to the boil then simmer for 30 minutes. Strain off the gravy and reserve and leave the meat mixture to get cold. Set oven to 375°F or Mark 5. Roll out the pastry on a lightly floured surface and use to line 8 small greased ramekin dishes, reserving approximately half the pastry for the lids. Divide the meat mixture evenly between the pies. Skim any fat from the top of the gravy and put 1 dessertspoonful into each pie. Dampen the lids, place on the pies, crimp the edges and make a steam hole in the centre of each. Brush well with beaten egg. Bake for 35 to 40 minutes or until the pastry is crisp and golden. Very carefully remove the pies from the dishes and place on a wire rack. Heat the remaining gravy and pour a little into each pie through the steam hole. Serve hot with potatoes and a green vegetable, or cold with pickles.

Beef Stew with Walnuts

A rich Berkshire stew.

1 lb stewing steak
1 oz dripping
1 onion, peeled and sliced
2 fl. oz red wine
1 pint beef stock
Salt and black pepper

2 sprigs thyme and 4 sprigs
 parsley, tied together with string
12 button mushrooms, wiped
2 oz chopped walnuts
1 stick of celery, trimmed and chopped
$\frac{1}{2}$ oz butter

A little grated orange peel for garnish

Cut the steak into 2 inch cubes, dust with a little seasoned flour and fry in the dripping until lightly browned. Remove with a slotted spoon and fry the onion in the residual dripping until golden. Return the meat to the pan and add the wine, stock, *bouquet garni* and seasoning. Bring to the boil, then cover and simmer for 1½ to 2 hours. Fry the mushrooms, walnuts and celery in the butter and add to the stew after 1 hour of cooking. Remove the herbs and transfer the stew to a heated serving dish. Serve, garnished with grated orange peel and accompanied by creamed potatoes and a green vegetable. Serves 4.

The Thames near Hurley

Buckingham Cakes

Small sponge cakes flavoured with ginger

2 eggs	½ teaspoon baking powder
4 oz butter	1 teaspoon ground ginger
4 oz caster sugar	1½ oz preserved ginger, finely chopped
4 oz flour	A little sifted icing sugar

Set oven to 375°F or Mark 5. Beat the eggs in a bowl set over a pan of warm water until fluffy. Cream the butter and sugar together until light and fluffy, then gradually beat in the eggs. Sift together the flour, baking powder and ground ginger and fold into the mixture, then fold in the preserved ginger. Spoon the mixture into buttered and floured patty tins and bake for 15 minutes, until golden and springy to the touch. Cool on a wire rack. Before serving, dust with sifted icing sugar. Makes between 12 and 16 cakes.

Devilled Mutton

A popular Victorian and Edwardian dish that was often served for breakfast. A Berkshire recipe using lamb, which is now more readily available.

8 slices cold roast lamb, thickly cut	**Juice of a lemon**
Salt and black pepper	**2 oz butter, melted**
$^1/_2$ teaspoon cayenne pepper	**4 oz lightly toasted breadcrumbs**
$^1/_2$ teaspoon dry English mustard	**Watercress or parsley for garnish**

Season the lamb slices with salt and pepper, cayenne pepper and mustard. Place in a shallow dish and pour over the lemon juice. Cover and leave to marinate for 30 minutes. Set oven to 375ºF or Mark 5. Remove the lamb slices from the marinade, brush with the melted butter and coat with breadcrumbs. Place in a greased roasting tin and bake for 15 minutes or until completely heated through. Serve garnished with watercress or parsley and accompanied by creamed potatoes and grilled tomatoes. Serves 4.

Quainton Village

Buckinghamshire Cherry Dumpers

Black Cherry orchards were once widespread in Buckinghamshire and on Cherry Pie Sunday, at the end of August when cherry picking was completed, these fruit turnovers were eaten. Traditionally they were accompanied by a tankard of ale.

1 lb black cherries, pitted.	**2 oz granulated sugar**
If tinned cherries used, ensure	**A little milk**
that they are well drained	**Caster sugar**
8 oz prepared shortcrust pastry	

Set oven to 400°F or Mark 6. Roll out the pastry on a lightly floured surface to about ⅛ inch thick and cut out 4 inch circles. Divide the cherries evenly between these, piling a few on each circle, then sprinkle over the granulated sugar. Dampen the edges of the circles with a little cold water and fold up into turnovers, pinching the edges firmly together. Brush with milk and place on a lightly greased baking sheet. Bake for 20 to 30 minutes or until golden, then sprinkle with caster sugar while still hot. Serve hot or cold.

Oxford Sausages

The recipe for these skinless sausages dates back to the 18th century.

1 lb lean boneless pork
1 lb lean boneless veal
12 oz shredded suet
8 oz fresh white breadcrumbs
Grated rind of half a lemon
1 teaspoon ground nutmeg

1 tablespoon chopped mixed fresh
   parsley, thyme, mint and marjoram
1 teaspoon chopped fresh sage
Salt and black pepper
1 egg, beaten
A little flour

Mince or *very* finely chop the pork and veal. Place in a large bowl and add the suet, breadcrumbs, lemon rind, nutmeg and all the herbs. Mix well together and season. Add the egg and stir well until the mixture is well combined and bound together. Flour the hands and form the mixture into sausage shapes. Dust lightly with flour and either cook the sausages under a hot grill, turning frequently until brown and cooked through, or fry in a mixture of oil and butter for about 8 minutes, turning frequently. Serve with creamed potatoes, grilled tomatoes and bacon. Makes approx. 24 sausages.

Gammon and Apricot Pie

The combination of gammon or ham with apricots dates back at lest to Elizabethan days. This recipe is from Buckinghamshire.

4 gammon steaks,
   approx. 1 inch thick
1 to 1¹/₂ oz butter
5 oz dried apricots
   (the no-soak type are ideal)

Black pepper
¹/₂ oz sultanas
¹/₂ pint pork stock
1 to 1¹/₂ lb potatoes, peeled and
   parboiled, then cut into slices

Set oven to 350°F or Mark 4. Fry the gammon lightly on both sides in half the butter. Arrange in a 1½ to 2 pint pie dish and cover with the apricots. Season lightly with pepper, then sprinkle over the sultanas. Pour on the stock and cover the filling with overlapping layers of potatoes. Melt the remaining butter and brush over the potatoes. Cover the pie with a piece of kitchen foil and bake for 1 hour then remove the foil and bake for a further 20 to 30 minutes to brown the potatoes. Serve with carrots and peas. Serves 4.

Windsor Tartlets

A recipe from the 19th century, when figs were a popular dried fruit.

4 oz flour	2 oz candied lemon peel,
2 oz butter, softened	finely minced
1 egg yolk, beaten	1 teaspoon lemon juice
2 oz dried figs, very	4 oz apricot jam
finely chopped	1 egg, beaten
2 oz ground almonds	Additional apricot jam

A little caster sugar

Sift the flour into a bowl, then rub in the butter and bind the mixture with beaten egg yolk to form a soft dough. Chill for 15 to 20 minutes. Set oven to 375°F or Mark 5. Roll out the pastry thinly on a lightly floured surface and use to line 12 to 14 greased tartlet tins, trimming the edges neatly. Mix together the figs, ground almonds, lemon peel, lemon juice, jam and beaten egg, combining well. Place a little of the additional apricot jam in the base of each pastry case and divide the filling between them. Smooth over and sprinkle with a little caster sugar. Bake for 15 to 20 minutes until golden. Cool in the tins for 2 minutes, then place on a wire rack.

Windsor Castle from the Thames

Eton Mess

*Named after Eton College, this is a delicious summer dessert of
strawberries, meringues and cream.*

2 large egg whites	**2 lb fresh strawberries washed,**
4 oz caster sugar	**drained well and hulled**
1 oz icing sugar, sifted	**3 tablespoons brandy**
³/₄ pint double cream	

Set oven to 250ºF or Mark ½. Whisk the egg whites in a clean, grease free bowl, until they are stiff enough not to fall out of the bowl when it is turned upside down. Add half the sugar and whisk in well, then fold in the remaining sugar. Using a tablespoon, drop even piles of the meringue mixture on to a lightly greased baking sheet. Bake for 1½ hours or until the meringues are a light cream colour with a slightly soft centre. Cool on a wire rack. Reserving a few strawberries for decoration, roughly chop up the remainder, put into a bowl and sprinkle over them the icing sugar and brandy. Chill for 1 to 2 hours. Whip the cream until it just holds its shape and carefully fold in the strawberries and their liqueur. Crush the meringues and fold into the strawberry mixture. Pile into a glass dish and decorate with the reserved strawberries. Serves 4 to 6. If preferred, shop-bought meringues can be used, though home-made ones are nicer.

Orange Tart

Queen Charlotte, wife of George III, was said to have been particularly fond of this dessert; the recipe comes from an 18th century Oxford manuscript.

8 oz prepared shortcrust pastry   **5 oz caster sugar**
Finely grated rind of 3 oranges   **3 tablespoons cornflour**
Grated rind and juice of 1 lemon   **5 eggs, separated**
Juice of 3 oranges made up to 14 fl.oz with fresh orange juice

Set oven to 400ºF or Mark 6. Roll out the pastry on a lightly floured surface and use to line a greased 9 inch flan tin, trimming the edges neatly. Bake blind for 15 to 20 minutes. In a bowl, mix together the orange and lemon rind, then add the orange juice and stir in 4 oz of the sugar. Blend in the cornflour and pour the mixture into a saucepan. Bring to the boil, stirring, then reduce the heat and cook, still stirring, for 1 minute until smooth and thickened. Remove from the heat and stir in the lemon juice. Beat the egg yolks together and fold into the mixture. Pour into the flan case. Lower the oven temperature to 300ºF or Mark 2. Whisk the egg whites with the remaining 1 oz of sugar until they stand up in stiff peaks. Pile or pipe the egg whites on the filling, covering it completely and bake for 30 minutes until the meringue is crisp and lightly golden. Serve hot or cold. Serves 4 to 6.

At Burnham Beeches

Buckinghamshire Rabbit Pie

A puff pastry pie with rabbit, cheese, macaroni and double cream.

A 2 to 2½ lb rabbit, jointed
A bouquet garni
1 onion peeled, whole and
   stuck with 6 cloves
Salt and black pepper
2 oz short cut macaroni

1 small onion, peeled and
   finely chopped
2 oz Cheddar cheese, grated
2 teaspoons chopped fresh parsley
1 teaspoon chopped fresh thyme
½ pint double cream

8 oz prepared puff pastry   A little beaten egg

Soak rabbit joints in cold salted water for 1½ hours. Drain well. Place in saucepan, cover with fresh water and bring to boil. Skim, then add the *bouquet garni*, onion and seasoning. Cover and simmer for 1 to 1½ hours, until rabbit is tender. Remove rabbit and strain and reserve stock. Cool slightly, then remove meat from bones. Bring reserved stock to boil and add macaroni. Boil until tender, then drain macaroni and mix with rabbit meat. Stir in onion, grated cheese and herbs and season. Turn rabbit mixture into 2 pint pie dish and place pie funnel in centre. Pour over cream. Set oven to 425°F or Mark 7. Roll out pastry and cut off narrow band. Line rim of pie dish, brush with cold water and top with remaining pastry. Cut two steam vents, then brush with beaten egg. Bake for 40 minutes or until golden brown. Serve with creamed potatoes and carrots. Serves 4 to 6.

Duke of Windsor's Gingerbread

This gingerbread was reputed to have been a favourite with the Duke of Windsor, later Edward VIII, when he was a child.

8 oz flour	4 oz almonds, chopped
4 oz butter	1 oz mixed candied peel, chopped
4 oz soft brown sugar	8 oz black treacle, warmed
1/2 oz ground ginger	1/4 teaspoon bicarbonate of soda
1/2 teaspoon ground allspice	1 egg

2 tablespoons milk

Set oven to 350°F or Mark 4. Sift the flour into a bowl, then rub in the butter until the mixture resembles fine breadcrumbs. Stir in the sugar, spices, chopped blanched almonds and chopped peel. Mix the treacle and bicarbonate of soda together and beat into the mixture. Beat the egg and milk together and stir into the mixture, combining well. Pour into a greased and floured 2 lb loaf tin and bake for 40 minutes. Cool in the tin for 5 minutes, then turn out on to a wire rack. Serve sliced and spread with butter.

Pancakes

The Buckinghamshire town of Olney is famous for its Shrove Tuesday Pancake Race, said to have its origins in the 14th century, when a housewife, frying pancakes, heard the church bell ring and, not wanting to be late for the service, ran to church, frying pan in hand and still wearing her apron.

3 oz flour	**½ pint milk**
Pinch of salt	**1 to 2 oz melted butter**
3 eggs	**Lemon juice and caster sugar**

Lemon slices for decoration

Sift the flour and salt together into a bowl. Make a well in the centre and add the eggs, beating well. Then gradually stir in the milk, beating until a smooth, creamy batter is formed. Leave the batter to stand in a cool place for 10 to 15 minutes. Grease an omelette or frying pan with butter and heat until smoking hot. Stir the melted butter into the batter and spoon in enough batter to coat the pan lightly. Cook for about ½ minute until lightly set on top and golden underneath, then toss or turn with a palette knife, to cook the topside. Cooking only takes about 1 minute. Sprinkle the pancake with lemon juice and sugar, roll up or fold into a triangle and serve immediately from the pan, decorated with a slice of lemon. Make the remainder of the pancakes in the same way, serving them piping hot. Serves 4.

METRIC CONVERSIONS

The weights, measures and oven temperatures used in the preceding recipes can be easily converted to their metric equivalents. The conversions listed below are only approximate, having been rounded up or down as may be appropriate.

Weights

Avoirdupois	Metric
1 oz.	just under 30 grams
4 oz. (¼ lb.)	app. 115 grams
8 oz. (½ lb.)	app. 230 grams
1 lb.	454 grams

Liquid Measures

Imperial	Metric
1 tablespoon (liquid only)	20 millilitres
1 fl. oz.	app. 30 millilitres
1 gill (¼ pt.)	app. 145 millilitres
½ pt.	app. 285 millilitres
1 pt.	app. 570 millilitres
1 qt.	app. 1.140 litres

Oven Temperatures

	°Fahrenheit	Gas Mark	°Celsius
Slow	300	2	150
	325	3	170
Moderate	350	4	180
	375	5	190
	400	6	200
Hot	425	7	220
	450	8	230
	475	9	240

Flour as specified in these recipes refers to plain flour unless otherwise described.